The Night *Dragon*

written by Joelie Croser
illustrated by Donna Gynell

Chapter 1

Bang! Boom! Doof!

There was a knocking on the window. Toby woke up in fright.

Bang! Boom! Doof!

"There it is again," he said. "It sounds like a dragon, and it's trying to come in!"

Toby sat up in bed. How could he sleep with a dragon outside his window?

Bang! Boom! Doof! The knocking was louder.

"That dragon must have big feet," said Toby. Then he grabbed his pillow and squeezed it hard. "I hope the window is strong," he thought. "It must be really strong to keep out a dragon with big feet."

Bang! Boom! Doof!

This time it was
even louder! And
the knocking sound
seemed higher up
on the window.
Maybe the dragon
was trying to fly in!

"I wonder if it's
a fire-breathing
dragon," whispered
Toby. And he
squeezed his pillow even harder as he
stared out into the darkness. "It might
start breathing fire any minute."

Chapter 2

Outside on the garden path sat a big, green frog. He was on his way to the pond in Toby's garden. But instead of jumping from bush to bush down to the water, he kept jumping into a wall. It was an invisible wall.

"I can smell the water," said the frog. "I can hear the water. But can I get to the water? No!"

The frog went back a few steps and tried again. Hop, hop, hop he went. Then he jumped, higher and harder than ever.

Bang! Boom! Doof! The wall that he could not see was still there. His chin hurt from crashing into it. His tummy and his four big feet were hurting, too.

"One more try," sighed the frog. "If I can't get over this wall with one more jump, I'll just have to go back to my other pond."

He hopped back up the path to get ready for one last jump.

Chapter 3

"That's enough!" said Toby when he heard the last sounds. "I can't sit here hiding behind my pillow all night. I'll find out what kind of dragon it is."

Toby crept over to his desk. He opened a drawer and felt around for something.

Meanwhile, he could hear some small tapping sounds on the ground outside. Maybe the dragon was shaking itself and some of its scales were falling out like dog hair!

Toby found what he wanted. He crept past his bed and gave his pillow a pat for good luck. Then he went boldly over to the window and waited for the sound.

Bang! Boom! Doof! There it was!

Toby switched on the flashlight that he held in his hand, and there, on the window, was the thing that had made´ the noise.

"It's only a frog!" laughed Toby as he let the flashlight shine all around it.

Chapter 4

"Aaah!" cried the frog as it stuck to the glass. "First there is a wall I can't see, and now there is a fire-breathing dragon. I'm going back to the other pond!"